ENOS SLAUGHTER

RAY LANKFORD

OZZIE SMITH

ROGERS HORNSBY

LOU BROCK

ALBERT PUJOLS

FRANKIE FRISCH

WILLIE McGEE

DIZZY DEAN

STAN MUSIAL

BOB GIBSON

MARK McGWIRE

THE HISTORY OF THE
ST. LOUIS CARDINALS

MICHAEL E. GOODMAN

CREATIVE ✺ EDUCATION

Published by Creative Education, 123 South Broad Street, Mankato, MN 56001

Creative Education is an imprint of The Creative Company.

Designed by Rita Marshall.

Photographs by AllSport (Brian Bahr, Otto Greule, Elsa Hasch), Associated Press/Wide World Photos,

Icon Sports Media (John Biever), The Sporting News Archive, SportsChrome (Steven Goldstein,

Jonathan Kirn, Tony Tomsic, Rob Tringali Jr., Steve Woltman)

Library of Congress Cataloging-in-Publication Data

Goodman, Michael E. The history of the St. Louis Cardinals / by Michael Goodman.

p. cm. — (Baseball)   ISBN 1-58341-221-2

Summary: Highlights the key personalities and memorable games in the history of the

team that has won fifteen National League pennants and nine world championships,

second only to the New York Yankees, in the past one hundred years.

1. St. Louis Cardinals (Baseball team)—History—

Juvenile literature. [1. St. Louis Cardinals (Baseball team)—History.

2. Baseball—History.] I. Title. II. Baseball (Mankato, Minn.).

GV875.S74 G66 2002   796.357'64'0977866—dc21   2001047866

9 8 7 6 5 4 3

IN 1764,

A GROUP OF FRENCH FUR TRADERS SET OUT FROM

New Orleans to build a trading post where the Mississippi and

Missouri rivers met. They named the trading post St. Louis, after

Louis IX, a former French king. The little settlement was in an ideal

location to become the gateway to the American West. Pioneers

heading toward the Rockies and the Pacific coast bought their

supplies and began their journeys in St. Louis, while some travelers

stayed and helped build a thriving metropolis.

In 1876, more than 100 years after its founding, St. Louis

welcomed a new type of pioneer—one of the first professional

baseball teams in the United States. The team, originally known as

the Browns and later given the more colorful name Cardinals, has

GROVER ALEXANDER

had its own colorful history. Over the years, some of baseball's most

talented and entertaining players have put their skills on display in

the "Gateway City."

{**"THE RAJAH" REIGNS**} In 1876, the St. Louis

Browns became a charter member of the National

League (NL). The franchise switched to a league

called the American Association in the 1880s, winning

6   four consecutive league titles from 1885 to 1888. The Browns

rejoined the NL in the 1890s with a new name, the Perfectos, but

they were far from perfect. One year they lost a whopping 111

games, finishing in 12th place in the standings.

The year 1900 brought a new identity for the St. Louis

franchise. Club management decided to rename the team the

Cardinals and to replace its dull brown-and-white uniforms with

brighter red-and-white ones. The Cardinals remained near the

EDGAR RENTERIA

In **1922**, star Rogers Hornsby posted 42 homers, 152 RBI, and a .401 batting average.

ROGERS HORNSBY

bottom of the NL until the arrival of a skinny second baseman from

Texas in 1915. His name was Rogers Hornsby, but St. Louis fans

soon began calling him "the Rajah" because of the

way he ruled the batter's box. Hornsby built up his

muscles and quickly became the best hitter in the

league. During 23 big-league seasons, he topped

the .300 mark 21 times, hitting over .400 three of

Pitcher Jesse Haines made headlines in **1924** by throwing a no-hitter against the Red Sox.

those years. Hornsby's lifetime batting average of .358 is second only

to that of legendary Detroit Tigers outfielder Ty Cobb.

Strength was only one reason for Hornsby's success at the

plate. Dedication was another. He never drank or smoked and rarely

went out in public. He even refused to read books or go to the

movies, fearing these activities might damage his batting eye. "I am

only interested in being a great ballplayer," he once said. "Everything

else is of little concern to me."

JESSE HAINES

The Cardinals
moved into
Busch
Stadium,
their sixth
overall home,
in **1966**.

BUSCH STADIUM

In 1925, Hornsby took on a new role with the Cardinals when he was named player/manager. In his first year at the helm, the Rajah led the Cards from last place to fourth. The next season, he guided them to their first NL pennant.

In the 1926 World Series, the Cardinals faced the New York Yankees and their famous "Murderers' Row" lineup, which was led by powerful hitters Babe Ruth and Lou Gehrig. But the Yankees were no match for St. Louis pitcher Grover Cleveland Alexander. The 39-year-old ace won games two and six and then relieved St. Louis starter Jesse Haines in the seventh inning of the final game to preserve the victory and the Cards' first world championship.

{DIZZY AND THE "GAS HOUSE GANG"} The next year, Hornsby was traded to the New York Giants for second baseman Frankie Frisch. It was the first step in building one of the most tal-

DIZZY DEAN

ented and unusual teams in baseball history. No club has had more

genuine characters than the Cardinals of the 1930s. Among those

memorable players were Frisch, pitcher Dizzy Dean and his brother

Paul (whose nickname was "Daffy"), third baseman Pepper Martin,

and shortstop Leo "the Lip" Durocher. They played the game with

reckless abandon and didn't mind getting dirty. In fact, their grimy uniforms earned them the nickname the "Gas House Gang."

Dizzy Dean was the fans' favorite. He loved to boast about his

St. Louis star Frankie Frisch hit a home run in the very first All-Star Game, held in **1933**. ability, but he always seemed able to live up to his bragging. Before one game against the Boston Braves, he paraded in front of the opponents' dugout and announced, "I'm throwing nothing but fastballs at you, sonnies. You don't have to worry about Ol' Diz's curve

today." He was true to his word, but even knowing what was coming, the Braves managed only three weak hits.

Before the 1934 season, Dizzy boasted that he and his brother Paul would win 45 games and lead the Cardinals to a World Series title. In fact, the brothers won 49 games (30 for Dizzy and 19 for Daffy) as the Cards won the NL crown. Each brother then defeated the Detroit Tigers twice during the World Series to make the Cards champions again.

DARRYL KILE

{STAN IS THE MAN} The Gas House Gang never again matched its 1934 performance, but St. Louis fans had lots to cheer about for the rest of the 1930s. Then the cheers turned to roars in

the 1940s. Between 1941 and 1949, the "Redbirds" never finished lower than second place in the league, winning four pennants and three World Series titles.

Many people consider the 1942 Cardinals one of the best NL squads ever. That team featured three outstanding youngsters: shortstop Marty Marion, right fielder Enos "Country" Slaughter, and left fielder Stan Musial. The club didn't have much power, but its speed and endless energy earned the players their own nickname: the "St. Louis Swifties." The Swifties sprinted to the finish line, winning 11 of their last 12 games to edge the Brooklyn Dodgers for the NL pennant. Then they routed the Yankees in five games in the World Series.

The Cards captured world championships in 1944 and 1946 as well. St. Louis fans will never forget the ending of the 1946 World Series against the Boston Red Sox, when Slaughter made a mad dash all the way home from first base on a single to score the go-ahead run in the seventh game.

Speedster Enos "Country" Slaughter was terrific in **1942**, leading the NL in hits (188) and triples (17).

ENOS SLAUGHTER

Like Stan Musial, **1990s** slugger Mark McGwire was known for his home run power.

The brightest star of that era in St. Louis was Musial, who continued to play outstanding ball in the 1950s and '60s. Perhaps no other NL player has been as consistently great for so long. That's why fans dubbed him "the Man." When the Cards needed a big hit, Stan was the man they turned to.

Musial was named the NL Most Valuable Player (MVP) in 1944, 1947, and 1948 and continued to smack hits and drive in runs for 22 seasons until he retired in 1963. He ended his career with 3,630 hits, a .331 lifetime batting average, and 475 home runs. In an interview in 1953, Hall of Fame outfielder Ty Cobb commented, "No man has ever been a perfect ballplayer. Stan Musial, however, is the closest thing to perfection in the game today. He's certainly one of the great hitters of all time."

{BOYER, BROCK, AND "BULLET BOB"} The year after Musial retired, he watched proudly as the Cardinals won the NL

The great Stan Musial played in 21 All-Star Games, the first in **1943** and the last in **1963**.

STAN MUSIAL

pennant in an exciting finish and then captured the World Series.

The 1964 champs were led by three very different players—third

baseman Ken Boyer, outfielder Lou Brock, and pitcher Bob Gibson.

Boyer, the team captain, was the leader on and off the field.

Whenever players needed advice or an example to follow, they

looked to Boyer. Brock, the NL's all-time stolen base leader, came to the Cardinals midway through the 1964 season in a trade with the

Chicago Cubs. He batted nearly .350 and stole 33 bases during his

first half-season in St. Louis and was a key part of the

Redbirds' NL-winning teams in 1967 and 1968.

St. Louis ace Bob Gibson was almost untouchable in **1968**, winning 15 consecutive games.

Gibson, meanwhile, was one of the greatest com-

petitors of all time. Batters respected his ability and

feared his fastball, which he often threw high and

tight. According to St. Louis catcher Tim McCarver, the Cardinals ace

was "far and away the meanest, nastiest pitcher I ever saw. There is no

second place on this list."

In 1968, "Bullet Bob" used his meanness to dominate the NL,

going 22–9 with an amazing 1.12 ERA. For his efforts, he was

named both league MVP and the Cy Young Award winner. Gibson

continued to star in St. Louis until 1975 and remains the club's

all-time leader in wins, shutouts, strikeouts, and innings pitched.

BOB GIBSON

Lou Brock led
St. Louis in
stolen bases
for 14 straight
seasons in
the **1960s**
and '**70s**.

LOU BROCK

{WHITEY AND "THE WIZARD"} After their great run in the 1960s, the Cardinals suffered a dry spell. Despite the outstanding hitting of Brock, third baseman Joe Torre, and first baseman Keith Hernandez, the Redbirds failed to capture a pennant during the 1970s.

John Tudor hurled 10 shutouts during the **1985** season as the Cards won their 14th NL pennant.

The Cards' fortunes turned around in the 1980s, though, with the arrival of manager Whitey Herzog and such key players as outfielder Willie McGee, shortstop Ozzie Smith, and pitchers John Tudor and Bruce Sutter. Herzog pushed and prodded the Redbirds to NL pennants in 1982, 1985, and 1987, and a world championship in 1982. They used a balance of timely offense, solid pitching, and amazing defense, especially by Ozzie Smith. After the 1982 championship, Herzog praised the "Wizard of Oz," claiming that "Ozzie took two hits or a run away from our opponents every game this year."

JOHN TUDOR

In the late 1980s, the team started to slip in the NL standings, and Herzog was replaced by former Cardinals star Joe Torre. Torre engineered several key trades and gave added playing time to such

youngsters as catcher Tom Pagnozzi, outfielder Ray Lankford, and third baseman Todd Zeile. Torre also helped rebuild the confidence of veteran pitchers Bob Tewksbury and Lee Smith. The rejuvenated

Cards consistently finished high in the NL Eastern Division standings in the early 1990s.

But after the Redbirds posted a disappointing 62–81 record in 1995, team owners decided more changes were needed. Torre was replaced by Tony La Russa, who had led the Oakland A's to several American League pennants. Under La Russa, the Cards reached the playoffs in 1996 for the first time in 10 years. Leading the way were the league's best outfield trio—Lankford, Brian Jordan, and Ron Gant—and pitchers Alan Benes and Dennis Eckersley.

Defensive marvel Ozzie Smith earned 11 straight Gold Glove awards (from **1982** to **1992**).

{**"BIG MAC" SETS OFF FIREWORKS**} The Cardinals posted a disappointing 73–89 mark in 1997. Still, the Cardinals made a major improvement by trading for baseball's most powerful slugger, first baseman Mark McGwire, in midseason. McGwire, who had already hit 34 homers for Oakland before the trade, hit 24

OZZIE SMITH

more in St. Louis to finish with 58. And the long-ball fireworks were just beginning.

28

Center fielder Ray Lankford was strong at the plate in **1997**, driving in a career-best 98 runs.

"Big Mac" started the 1998 season by hitting a grand slam on opening day. Then he kept smacking the ball out of the yard. Fans around the country watched breathlessly as McGwire and Cubs slugger Sammy Sosa both attempted to eclipse Roger Maris's record of 61 homers in a season. Both easily surpassed Maris and continued dueling for the home run title. By season's end, McGwire outslugged Sosa 70–66 and became the first player ever to hit 50-plus home runs in three straight years.

McGwire made it four in a row in 1999 by smashing 65 homers, but the Cards were winners only at the ticket office, setting franchise attendance records. To improve on the team's 75–86 record, St. Louis management decided to get McGwire some help.

RAY LANKFORD

Soon, center fielder Jim Edmonds, shortstop Edgar Renteria, catcher

Mike Matheny, and pitchers Darryl Kile and Pat Hentgen arrived in

St. Louis, helping the Cards post a division-winning

95–67 record in 2000. The club then swept the

favored Atlanta Braves in the playoffs before falling to

the New York Mets in the NL Championship Series.

In **1999**, outfielder Fernando Tatis made big-league history with two grand slams in one inning.

After the season, Edmonds and Matheny earned

Gold Gloves for their fielding, and Kile—the team's first 20-game

winner in 15 years—placed high in the voting for the Cy Young

Award. The improvements continued the following year, when

exciting rookie third baseman Albert Pujols joined the club and

helped the Redbirds make the playoffs again. Although McGwire

brought his Hall of Fame career to an end at the conclusion of the

2001 season, the Cardinals adjusted to the loss by signing Tino

Martinez, a longtime star first baseman for the New York Yankees.

FERNANDO TATIS

A defensive standout, veteran outfielder Jim Edmonds also wielded a booming bat.

JIM EDMONDS

Young third baseman Albert Pujols exploded for 130 RBI during the **2001** season.

ALBERT PUJOLS

Like their predecessors in red and white, today's Cardinals are

a perennial force in the National League. With the Cardinals

building on a winning tradition forged in the Gateway City for

more than 120 years, St. Louis fans have good reason to believe

that their team's future will remain as bright as its uniforms.